P9-AOE-020

SPORTS BIOGRAPHIES

ALEX MORGAN

KENNY ABDO

Fly!
An Imprint of Abdo Zoom
abdobooks.com

abdobooks.com

Published by Abdo Zoom, a division of ABDO, P.O. Box 398166, Minneapolis, Minnesota 55439.

Printed in the United States of America, North Mankato, Minnesota.
052020
092020

Photo Credits: AP Images, Getty Images, Icon Sportswire, iStock, Kelley L Cox, newscom, Shutterstock, ©rachael.c.king p15 / CC BY 2.0
Production Contributors: Kenny Abdo, Jennie Forsberg, Grace Hansen
Design Contributors: Dorothy Toth, Neil Klinepier

Library of Congress Control Number: 2019956192

Publisher's Cataloging-in-Publication Data

Names: Abdo, Kenny, author.
Title: Alex Morgan / by Kenny Abdo
Description: Minneapolis, Minnesota : Abdo Zoom, 2021 | Series: Sports biographies | Includes online resources and index.
Identifiers: ISBN 9781098221362 (lib. bdg.) | ISBN 9781098222345 (ebook) | ISBN 9781098222833 (Read-to-Me ebook)
Subjects: LCSH: Morgan, Alex (Alexandra Patricia), 1989---Juvenile literature. | Professional athletes--United States--Biography--Juvenile literature. | Soccer players--United States--Biography--Juvenile literature. | Women soccer players--Biography--Juvenile literature.
Classification: DDC 796.334092 [B]--dc23

TABLE OF CONTENTS

ALEX MORGAN

Dominating the soccer field, Alex Morgan achieved superstar status at a very young age.

LIVING
FOOTBALL
FIFA
USA

USA
17

The star **forward** is a fighter on and off of the field. Morgan is one of the top goal scorers in the league. She also works against **wage discrimination** between male and female athletes.

EARLY YEARS

Alex Morgan was born in San Dimas, California, in 1989.

Morgan excelled at many sports in high school. She didn't start playing soccer until she was 14. Morgan was high school All-American and a three-time all-league pick.

Morgan went to the University of California at Berkeley. She led the team to the NCAA Tournament in all four of her years. But the furthest they **advanced** was to the second round.

Cal
13

GOING PRO

In 2011, Morgan was drafted by the Western New York Flash. She was also on US women's national soccer team (USWNT) in the 2011 **FIFA Women's World Cup.**

Morgan moved to the Seattle Sounders in 2012. Then she joined the Portland Thorns football **club** (FC) in 2013. She won the **inaugural** NWSL **Championship** that year.

13
13

At the 2012 Summer **Olympic Games**, Morgan won her first Olympic gold medal. US beat Japan 2–1. Watched by more than 80,000 people, it was the largest soccer crowd in Olympics history.

CANADA
2015
FIFA
FIFA

Morgan went into the 2015 **FIFA World Cup** with a knee injury. But she returned to the starting lineup and helped the US women claim their first World Cup **title** since 1999.

USA
13
WAY
adidas

Morgan was co-captain of Team USA at the 2019 World Cup. The team pulled away for a 2-0 win and their fourth World Cup **title**!

LEGACY

Morgan won the Adidas **Silver Boot** in the Women's **FIFA World Cup** in 2019. She won best female athlete at the ESPY awards that same year.

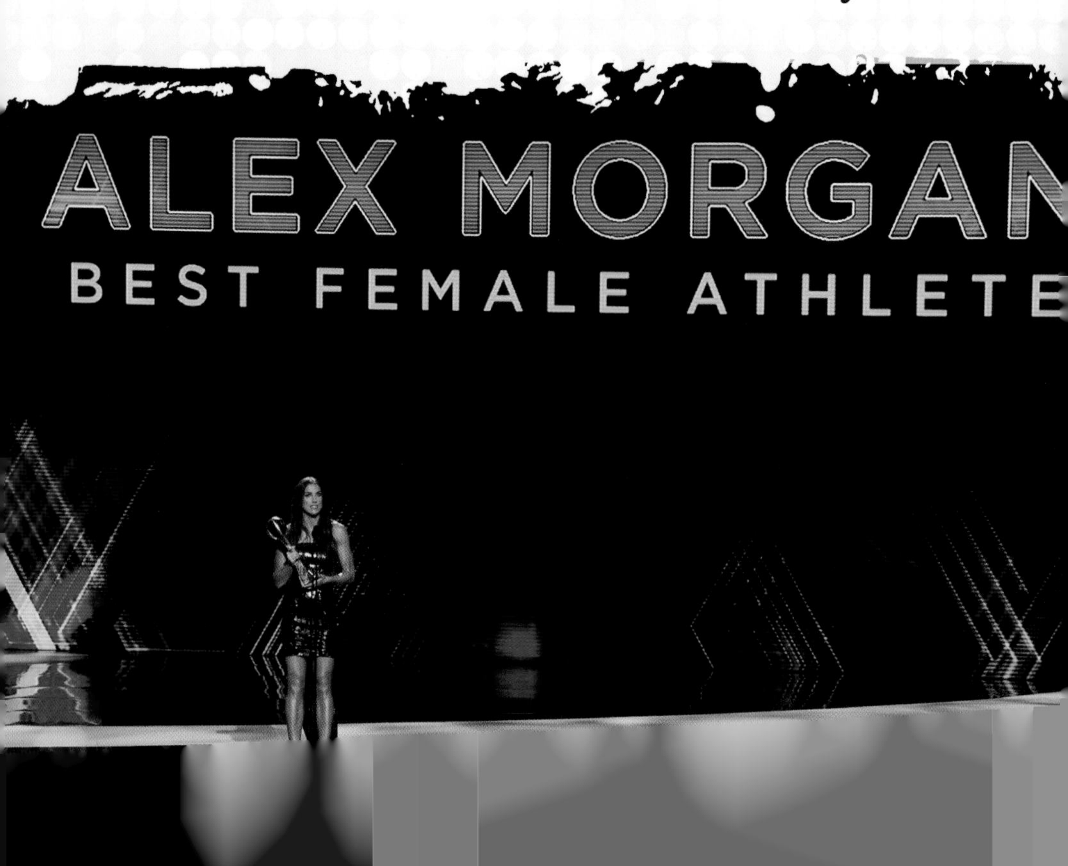

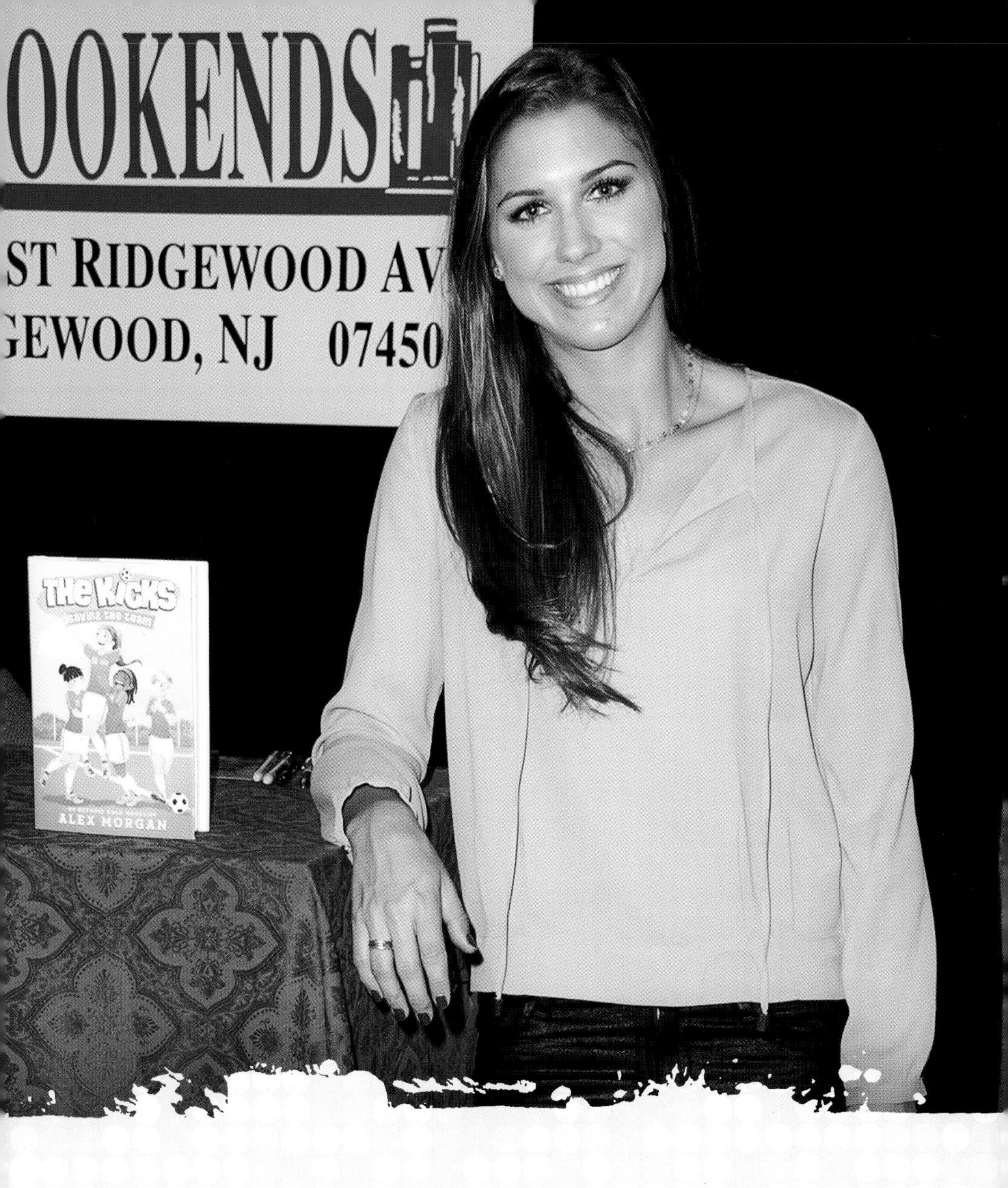

Morgan wrote a series of soccer-themed children's books in 2012. Her book *The Kicks: Saving the Team* was a *New York Times* bestseller! It was **adapted** into a TV show in 2015.

GLOSSARY

adaptated – changed for a particular use, like from a book to a movie.

advance – to move forward.

championship – a game held to find a first-place winner.

club – a group of people dedicated to one soccer team.

FIFA World Cup – an international soccer competition held every four years.

forward – an athlete on a soccer team that plays closest to the opponent's goal.

inaugural – the first or beginning of an activity.

Olympic Games – the biggest sporting event in the world that is divided into summer and winter games.

Silver Boot – an award given to second-placed players in the FIFA Women's World Cup.

title – a first-place position in a contest.

ONLINE RESOURCES

To learn more about Alex Morgan, please visit **abdobooklinks.com** or scan this QR code. These links are routinely monitored and updated to provide the most current information available.

INDEX